TRAIL DUST

COWBOYS, CATTLE AND COUNTRY

•

THE ART OF

James Reynolds

TRAIL

"The West endures like the prairie wind, and like the spirit of those willing to accept the challenge of life in a land that holds both promise and threat. This is a place where hardship and struggle are as surely certain as surroundings of splendid beauty."

DUST

COWBOYS, CATTLE AND COUNTRY

•

THE ART OF

James Reynolds

Text by
DON HEDGPETH

Introduction by
ELMER KELTON

•

THE GREENWICH WORKSHOP PRESS

To the Cowboy

*To those artists who have inspired me, to my friends and loved ones
who have supported me and especially to the cowboys, who have made the subject
matter of my paintings for the last forty years so much fun.*

A GREENWICH WORKSHOP PRESS BOOK

Inquiries should be addressed to The Greenwich Workshop, Inc., One Greenwich Place, P.O. Box 875, Shelton, Connecticut 06484-0875. Distributed to the trade by Artisan, A Division of Workman Publishing, 708 Broadway, New York, NY 10003.

Library of Congress Cataloging-in Publication Data:
Hedgpeth, Donald.

Traildust : cowboys, cattle, and country, the art of James Reynolds / text by Don Hedgpeth : introduction by Elmer Kelton.   p.   cm.   Includes index.
ISBN 0-86713-035-0 (hardcover : alk. paper).
1. Reynolds, James, 1926–   —Themes, motives.
2. Cowboys in art.   3. West (U.S.)—In art.
4. West (U.S.)—History.   I. Reynolds, James, 1926– .
II. Title.
ND237.R415A4   1997   759. 13—dc21
97-15123 CIP

For information about the limited edition prints, fine art lithography and canvas prints of James Reynolds, please write to The Greenwich Workshop, Inc., at the above address, or call 1-800-577-0666 (in the U.S.) to be connected with the authorized Greenwich Workshop dealer nearest you.

FRONTIS ART

2–3: Detail from *The Changeover*—Travel in the early West was a matter of endurance. Fresh horses will help to outrun the approaching storm. ■ 4–5: Detail from *Lee Mountain, Sedona, Arizona*—The sight of mountains stirs the soul. There is abundant inspiration here for artists and dreamers. ■ 6–7: Detail from *Another Time*—Longhorn cattle and dreamers on horseback, adrift upon a vast sea of grass along a trail into history.

•

Book design by Peter Landa and Judy Turziano
Calligraphy by Philip Bouwsma
Manufactured in Japan by Toppan Printing Co., Ltd.
First Printing 1997
97 98 99 0 9 8 7 6 5 4 3 2 1

CONTENTS

INTRODUCTION

Some regard the cowboy as a myth, a product of our effort to romanticize our past and create heroes who never existed because we seem to recognize so few in real life. A great deal of myth has grown up about the cowboy, but he was and still is a living, breathing reality. He is a skilled working man whose good fortune it is to do much of his work a-horseback on the open plains, in the mountains or in the borderland *brasada* of cactus and mesquite.

I was born into a family of cowboys and have spent my life around them. For a hundred years, various observers have proclaimed them extinct, but they remain alive and well though diminished in number. The art of James Reynolds and the prose of Don Hedgpeth present the cowboy as he has been and as he is today, changing as times change and technology advances, yet retaining many elements which first fired the American imagination in the traildrive years that followed the Civil War.

The cowboy arose out of necessity in a time when horizons were rapidly expanding. His cultural ancestors were Spanish herdsmen who sailed to the new world with Coronado and other conquistadors and adapted to a challenging open-range environment on the vast grazing lands of Mexico. From the Mexican vaquero came the American cowboy's basic working techniques, spreading from Texas northward to the high plains and the mountain states.

What was it about the early cowboy that so gripped the fancy first of Americans, then of the world? A major factor was the perception of his freedom. In truth, of course, that freedom had limitations. The cowboy, after all, was and is usually in someone else's employ, obliged to carry out the chores assigned to him if he expects to keep his job. However, he has always felt that he is free to draw his pay and ride away at will. The old-time cowboy had a reputation for drifting often from job to job, from one range to another. Many took pride in having worked from the Rio Grande to the Canadian line.

Since the ancient age of knighthood, popular imagination has

given the man on horseback superiority over the man on foot. This has lent to the aura that surrounds the cowboy. It is no accident that Zane Grey named one of his most popular Western novels *Knights of the Range*, a recognition of cowboy mythology. Yet, behind that myth, the man has always been real.

His workday, as Reynolds's paintings and drawings show, is usually long, starting at first daylight and lasting until the light is gone. From boyhood on a West Texas ranch, I can remember my father getting us up at four or five in the morning to eat a quick breakfast, saddle our horses and ride several miles to the back of a large pasture, then having to wait for sunrise so we could see the cattle we were supposed to gather. It might have been sundown or later before we unsaddled for the last time and trooped to the house or the chuck wagon for supper.

The work varied from day to day, season to season, so it was seldom monotonous for long. In spring and fall came branding and shipping, in summertime roping and doctoring, in wintertime feeding. Unpredictable horses and wild-natured cattle lent a degree of surprise and suspense even when the work itself descended into drudgery. And work it was, often too hot or too cold, too dry or too wet, too dusty or too deep in mud. It led to bruises and contusions, and occasionally worse. The pay was too small for the skill and responsibility required, the hazards involved.

Yet, remembering, I tend to shut out the negative, dwelling instead upon the fun, the camaraderie, the fresh air and golden sunshine, the challenges and the thrill of meeting them, or at least of trying. Most old cowboys I ever knew saw their life in the same terms. Many moved on to better-paying occupations under the pressures of family responsibilities, yet, with few exceptions, they still gloried in the memories of their cowboy days.

Those memories are stirred afresh in the art of James Reynolds and the prose of Don Hedgpeth, who understand the myth but show us the reality.
                                                                —ELMER KELTON

SIX-GUN MYTHS AND BOWLEGGED REALITY

"I have seen a cowboy come riding hard, full tilt down a steep, rocky slope, close behind a wild cow ducking and dodging in full flight. It was a rare glimpse of pure reckless abandon. As I watched nearby from the back of my own horse, my heart pumped faster and I could hear the blood pounding in my ears. I would not have traded places with anyone in the world during that brief, fleeting moment."

PART I

SIX-GUN MYTHS AND BOWLEGGED REALITY

Contemplating

There are moments to consider the blessings of another day:
horses to ride, a job to do, and a friend to share it with.
The future will take care of itself.

The prairie wind is like something alive and eternal. The grass sways in its currents as waves upon a vast rolling ocean. Along the faint trace of an old trail, dust drifts up into a bold blue sky that stretches taut toward distant horizons. Cattle graze across the grassy plain, and a solitary coyote prowls silently through the sage in the shadow of a hill. Off in the distance, skylined on a high mesa rim, a lone horseman comes riding. James Reynolds, an artist who paints the West, has known such scenes as this.

"I have seen a cowboy come riding hard, full tilt down a steep, rocky slope, close behind a wild cow ducking and dodging in full flight. It was a rare glimpse of pure reckless abandon. As I watched nearby from the back of my own horse, my heart pumped faster and I could hear the blood pounding in my ears. I would not have traded places with anyone in the world during that brief, fleeting moment."

It is a timeless tableau, isolated and remote from the modern world not only in terms of geography but also in spirit and tradition. This is the American West, once home to a proud race of hunters and warriors who lived in harmony with the land and were brothers to the wolf and eagle. Destiny had forever linked their fate to the great buffalo herds that thundered across the land in what surely seemed an infinite abundance. And so it had always been.

Something altered the harmony and natural balance of this world beginning in the middle of the sixteenth century. Up from the south

came Spanish adventurers lusting for empire and treasure. And where the intruder passed, the seeds of epic tragedy were scattered upon the prairie wind.

At the dawn of the nineteenth century, other strangers appeared at the fringe of the buffalo range. Like the Spaniards, these men also had ways that were a mystery to the native Americans. The vanguard came across the plains from the East and up the mighty river called Missouri. They were but a few at first: bold explorers and fur trappers, wilderness wanderers who posed no apparent threat to the native people of the prairie. But as time passed, more of them

Gate Shy

Range cattle may need to be penned during roundups in the spring or fall. After roaming free, they are reluctant to accept even temporary confinement.

came... and then still more, like an avalanche rolling and roaring down the steep slope of a mountainside.

Wagons strung out westward through the heart of the land toward the mountain barrier at the edge of the plains. Then trading

{19}

posts, military forts and small settlements sprang up like bitter weeds across the old trails of the buffalo. The discovery of gold in California at midcentury quickened the pace, and then came the trains following a pathway of promise that ran along shiny steel rails. Farmers plowed under the prairie grass, and Texas longhorn cattle crowded out the buffalo. For native Americans, the prelude to disaster had begun in earnest.

Blood and defiance were on the prairie wind from the end of the Civil War until the final decade of the century. The warrior's death song rose on that wind and echoed across the West, from the low hills of the Little Bighorn down into the desert stronghold of the fierce Apache. Many people believe that the West died in those lonely, desperate places. But it was not so. The West endures like the prairie wind and like the spirit of those willing to accept the challenge of life in a land that holds both promise and threat. This is a place where hardship and struggle are as surely certain as surroundings of splendid beauty.

The story of the West is a tale of triumph and tragedy with a full cast of characters, both heroes and villains, in the best tradition of classical drama. Indians and soldiers, trappers and trailblazers, miners and mule skinners, gunfighters and gamblers, homesteaders and sodbusters...all were players in the

The Big Move

Cowboys are hired men on horseback, and, although this scene depicts today, the nature of their work has changed little over the span of a century.

Sierra Packer

*A cowboy has to know his business when he's alone in the
high country that is summer range for cattle.
Self-reliance is a key to a lonely calling.*

pageant of the West. One figure stands out more starkly than all
the others, idealized and immortal in our collective consciousness:
the cowboy. He is a symbol of the idea of the West, both real and
imagined, forever riding wild and free across a prairie dreamscape.

Romantic fascination swirls around the cowboy and makes it difficult for us to see him clearly. Cowboy reality, both historical and contemporary, has been overwhelmed by a mythological haze of gun-
smoke and traildust. The truth is hard to get at and is not at all what
we imagine. The world laments a West that is not what it once had
been—when, in fact, it never really was.

The genesis of the American cowboy traces back through time and
across the broad ocean to Spain. Conquistadors, haughty and brave,

introduced cattle and horses to the New World when they landed on the shores of Mexico early in the sixteenth century. The Indians of Mexico became the first American cowboys. They adapted Spanish techniques of livestock management to new and diverse environments. Open-range cattle-raising became an economic cornerstone of the Spanish colonial empire, spreading throughout Mexico and into the American Southwest, particularly California and Texas.

The flavor and style of Spain were retained in the horseback heritage of California. But in Texas, Hispanic vaqueros and Anglo cow-

The Escort

In the beginning, white men were only travelers passing through the red man's domain. Where they paused, danger waited close by on the back of a painted pony.

boys developed their own way of doing things in response to the hard character of the country. Texas cowboys, Texas horses and Texas cattle set the style for the Western livestock industry on the

Great Plains east of the Rocky Mountains, from the Rio Grande north to the Canadian border.

The cowboy's golden age began in those dark days following the Civil War. As railroads built westward, shipping points were established in rough and rowdy Kansas cow towns like Dodge City and Abilene. Millions of Texas longhorn cattle followed the old trader's track called the Chisholm Trail northward across the Red River and on through the Indian Territory to the Kansas railheads…food for a war-weary, beef-hungry nation.

These were the glory days: a brief two dozen years when the cowboy captured the imagination of an entire world. They were wild rovers, horsemen daring and bold and, most of all, free and unfettered. Legend grew up along the cattle trail. The cowboy became

Packin' on the Flathead

Flathead Lake lies among the mountains in far northwest Montana. It is a sportman's paradise, where, today, packing in with horses adds an extra dimension to the adventure.

Cowboys and Indians

The story of conflict between cowboys and Indians was considerably less dramatic than the novels and movies would have us believe. Tensions existed, to be sure, and some blood was shed, but outright violence was rare.

During the open-range era of the cattle industry, the buffalo herds of the Great Plains had already reached the brink of extinction. Traildrivers moved their longhorn herds through a land tinged with the tragic plight of a once-mighty people. Cowboys cut out a few head of cattle as a toll for passage through Indian country and delivered entire herds on contract with the government to feed those tribes restricted to reservations. Cattlemen like Charles Goodnight, of Texas, negotiated private treaties with tribes such as the Comanche, and both sides were able to peacefully coexist.

It is perhaps ironic that most all Great Plains tribes are today involved in cattle ranching and that Indians have become some of the best cowboys that the  West can claim.

something more than what he really was…just a hired man on horseback charged with the welfare of the cattle that bore the boss's brand.

The modern age was dawning, and with it came the curses of crowded cities and industrialization. People bowed beneath the weight of drab, colorless lives marked by routine and monotony. There was enormous appeal in the romantic notion of the cowboy, a free-ranging rider galloping toward adventure in a land of high lonesome. The idea of such a figure provided a means of vicarious escape for all those who were trapped in bleak, ordinary lives. The popular press of the day, including newspapers, journals and pulp-fiction magazines, rushed to cash in on the public appetite. By the turn of the century, the cowboy had been transformed by printer's ink into a legendary character of such proportions as to rival the heroes of ancient mythology.

Three men played prominent roles in the creation of the cowboy legend. They were Owen Wister, Frederic Remington and Theodore Roosevelt. Wister created the prototypical cowboy myth when he published his enormously successful novel *The Virginian* in 1902. Wister's cowboy here was strong and laconic, honorable and gallant: chivalry incarnate, a knight on the Western plains. But there was little of cowboy reality in Wister's story—not even the presence of cattle. Morality was more important to Wister's Virginian than handling cattle and topping off broncs, and the gun replaced the lariat as the cowboy's favored tool.

Theodore Roosevelt had a genuine appetite for adventure and a zest for the rigorous life. As a young man, he briefly owned two ranches in the Dakota territories and reveled in the company of the cowboys who rode for his Elkhorn and Maltese Cross outfits. In later years, Roosevelt idealized his Dakota days. He wrote and spoke of the cowboys as men both primitive and noble. His cowboy memories were colored more by romantic notion than by rawhide reality. But he enjoyed a "bully pulpit" throughout his life, and the public believed him. After all, he had been there and they had not.

Frederic Remington had a major role in shaping the world's perception of cowboys. He, like Wister and Roosevelt, was an outsider, a visitor to the West whose experiences were transitory, and his observations superficial. Remington, in his art and his writings, showed us how cowboys *looked*, but not much about how they *were*. Visiting a cow camp is very different than living in one for a roundup season.

Wister, Roosevelt and Remington, taken together, exerted tremendous influence on the public through their separate and joint ventures, particularly in the popular press of the day. They created an image for the cowboy based on heroic drama, rather than the mundane reality of dirt, sweat and saddle sores. Buffalo Bill Cody and his

Chiricahua Stronghold

The Apache were a fierce, free people in a wild, daunting land: formidable foe to all who opposed them.

Wild West theatrical productions lent further substance to the myth, as did a booming market for pulp fiction featuring the exciting exploits of cowboy heroes based on Wister's Virginian.

Early in the century, the wilderness was fading fast and the nation hungered for a hero. The cowboy was chosen and thereby exiled to a romantic purgatory where he became a quixotic rider forever on the trail to glory. Few cared that he had survived the passing of the frontier era. Not all cowboys had died in stampedes on stormy nights, or been shot down on the dusty streets of Dodge or pierced through with Comanche arrows on a lonely stretch of prairie.

The world was rushing headlong into a new age in which there seemed no comfortable niche for a new generation of cowboys. Literature, and then the movies, relegated him to an earlier time. The cowboy became an icon of history but an outcast in the modern day. Americans still craved beef, everything from T-bone to hamburger,

Jack's Canyon (overleaf)

Wind and weather sweep down from the north. A cloudy vanguard announces the approaching storm in the red rock area of Sedona.

Cow Country

The word "country" has a particular meaning for people in the American West. It refers not to a specific geopolitical unit or nation, but rather to those regions of land suitable for ranching. "This is cow country!" has been the proud declaration for generations of families who have linked their fates to the risky venture of raising beef cattle.

High country, brush country, desert country...all identify the nature of different kinds of places where cattle are raised and cowboys are able to pursue their ambitions of working horseback. You will hear them talk about how dry it has been "over in my country," or that some rancher has just leased "a bunch of new country" on which to graze his cattle.

The success, or failure, of a ranching operation is tied to the condition of its "country." Being a good steward of his country is the primary consideration of any cattleman who expects to ride out the uncertainty of variables such as weather and the marketplace.

Colorado High Country

Near the mountains, cattle are grazing in the high country during the summer season, where melting snow nourishes the native grasses.

{31}

The Boss's Hoss

Each man is assigned a string of horses during roundup, and cowboys know not to mess with another man's mount—particularly if it belongs to the boss.

but seemed somehow unaware that the cattle business existed beyond Midwestern feedyards and the local butcher shop. Out West, sun and rain still nourished the prairie grass which sustained the grazing herds on ranches that were still run in the traditional manner…with those hired men on horseback, the cowboys. That they were ignored by the rest of the world bothered them not at all.

The concept of the cowboy as a legendary historical figure became even more entrenched through the movies. Hollywood exploited the appeal of the cowboy just as the popular press had in earlier years. William S. Hart was the first actor to make a career, and a fortune, through the fictional portrayal of the horseback hero battling the black-hatted forces of evil with blazing six-guns and a grim righteous determination.

Hollywood transformed the cowboy from a mounted herdsman to a warrior in the eternal conflict between good and evil. While the genuine article was still out there somewhere looking after cattle for pitiful wages, those who assumed and altered his true identity, through costume and dramatic contrivance, became rich. After Bill

Hart, an endless succession of actors put on big hats, boots and twin pistols in the continuing parody.

Generations of small boys sat in the Saturday afternoon darkness of movie theaters, entranced by the masquerade and caught up in a world of make-believe. Seasoned actors took on the identities of characters with names like Hopalong Cassidy, Lash LaRue, the Durango Kid and Red Ryder. Some spent their entire careers playing out the fantasy and working as pitchmen for a variety of products aimed at their audience of children. They were what we believed to be cowboys. But it was not true. Reality was far away from the footlights, out among the scrub and sage, where cold wind blew down the canyons and men rode out obscure lives defined by cow work and the cycle of seasons.

Cowboy reality was, and still is, a sharp-honed self-reliant attitude, a set of work skills, a strong sense of pride and loyalty, and an assortment of gear he calls an "outfit," which consists of a saddle, spurs, bridles, ropes, slicker, chaps, bedroll, boots, hat and a couple changes of clothes. Everything else that has attached itself to cowboys is incidental or imagined. The truth lies in the timeless natural chemistry of grass, rain, cattle, horses and men, a phenomenon based on mankind's natural appetite for beef. The cow is the critical core around which cowboy reality revolves.

After something close to a hundred years, chinks have begun to appear in the armor of myth surrounding the cowboy and the broader context of Western history. The world has discovered that there is still a real West: wild and wide-open places scarcely touched at all by the ravages of the modern age. And in those places, amazingly,

Members of the Board

On most Western ranches, the breeding bulls are kept separate from the cows, except in summer. This allows for an early spring calving season, hopefully after the last winter storm has blown itself out.

there are still some cowboys…like an ancient, extinct species rediscovered on a forgotten island in a remote corner of a faraway ocean.

Resurrection and renaissance are loose upon the tireless prairie wind… the cowboy lives—not next door, or down the block, but out there someplace uncrowded, comfortable in the company of his own kind. Most remarkable of all is that he is essentially the kind of man who inspired the myth a hundred years ago. And the American public is drawn to him for much the same reasons as in the beginning, before the myth took hold. The depersonalization of the computer age has cast a cloak of drab sameness upon

The Loner

Cowboys know about lonesome. To some, it is part of the attraction of the calling.

{35}

Stampede

They were, for the most part, young men…full and brimming over with life and a zest for their prairie adventure along the cattle trails. But terror ruled on those dark, stormy nights when the herd left the bedground and began to run.

"Stampede!" was the cry that froze the blood in a cowboy's veins as he rushed to his horse and spurred fast into the wild night. An old trail verse speaks of the dread that shadowed each man's heart:

O bury me not on the lone prairie,
Where coyotes howl and winds blow free.
In a narrow grave just six by three—
O bury me not on the lone prairie.

The White Man's Way

Death rode alongside men on the wild prairie. Indians and white men cultivated a stoic regard for the inevitable.

Reflectin'

A cowboy rests on a rim, scanning a canyon for cattle and perhaps reflecting on his love for this kind of life.

society just as did industrialization in an earlier time. The idea of a man on horseback in open country conjures up images of vitality and the kind of fierce individualism that is hard to achieve for the vast majority of people in today's world.

A cycle is complete. This century began with the genuine cowboy's being cast aside in favor of a mythological counterpart…and now, after almost a hundred years, reality has reclaimed the focus of our attention. American culture has recognized the false trappings of the cowboy of movies and popular fiction. We have reexamined the reality and found it every bit as appealing. Real cowboys have finally been represented truthfully in a profusion of books and movies, and in exhibitions of photography and fine art.

James Reynolds is a major force in the "Western Renaissance." His paintings are reflections of reality…cowboy reality: uncomplicated compositions of men and horses in a vastness of land and sky.

Reynolds has filtered out the pseudo-drama of whopping warriors and tight-eyed gunfighters. He has said, "Truth is an important element of my art. I have always tried to paint as honestly as I could. I don't embellish the fact that cowboy life is, for the most part, hours of monotony interrupted by brief intervals of high drama. I have been out there with those boys and have seen reality up close and from the back of a horse. And although it is not my reason for painting, I know that the body of my work is a documentation of cowboy life during this time. At some point in the future, people will be able to look at my painting and see how it once was out West, just as we do so today with Frederic Remington's work. I believe that my understanding of Western reality has strengthened my art. I was, like most people, drawn to cowboys as a result of the myth. But it is the reality that has sustained and held my interest, and been the inspiration for my art."

THE RANGE COUNTRY: LAND MADE FOR LEGEND

"The essence of the West remains constant. It is a big country beneath a big sky: a cowboy and Indian Valhalla of open plains and shining mountains where silence reigns when the prairie wind dies down. Isolation and loneliness haunt the quiet expanse like shadows across a panorama of natural splendor."

PART II
THE RANGE COUNTRY: LAND MADE FOR LEGEND

Summer Range

A cowboy needs but a few things to make him content: good horses to ride, cattle to care for and wide-open country far away from the crowds and concrete. The priorities have not changed . . . and it's not likely that they ever will.

{42}

James Reynolds
1981

The story of the West is a tale of man's response to the challenge of a land. The West is a real place, definable in the metes and bounds of geographers. It is also a fiery crucible within which history and legend were fused into an alloy of character that is uniquely American. Man did not shape the West; just the opposite is true. In this place, it was man who bent to the environment.

The essence of the West remains constant. It is a big country beneath a big sky: a cowboy and Indian Valhalla of open plains and shining mountains where silence reigns when the prairie wind dies down. Isolation and loneliness haunt the quiet expanse like shadows across a panorama of natural splendor. For artists and dreamers like James Reynolds, it is possible to discern ghosts of the past moving against a landscape that is virtually unchanged through time.

"Every aspect of the country interests me. When I first moved to Arizona from Los Angeles, it was hard to believe it was real. I had never seen air so fresh and clear. People had not cluttered it all up yet, and wherever you looked there was the feeling that you were seeing it just as the Indians had, or the pioneers, all those long years ago. I guess it is the space most of all that fascinates me. Up on the reservation, or out on a big ranch, my imagination runs wild, just like a kid. I can see an Apache warrior up among the rocks, or an old-time cowboy riding down a trail behind a bunch of longhorn cows. The land has been a force in shaping me as an artist. I will always be excited by space and distance."

There is some difficulty in pinning down a precise and commonly accepted definition of the American West. In the broadest terms, it is that area that begins on the west bank of the Mississippi River and

stretches to the Pacific Ocean, bounded by international borders on the north and south. Within that enormous geographical context are a number of distinct regions of remarkable diversity and contrasts.

Moving west...beyond the Mississippi valley, the rolling hills and trees give way to fertile flatlands from the Gulf coastal plain up to the eastern edge of the Dakotas. Then, around the ninety-eighth meridian, the prairies begin, that area that Conrad Richter called

High Prairie, Nevada

Cowboys in Nevada's high desert ranges are called "buckeroos," from the Spanish word "vaqueros." They are distinctive in their manner of dress and equipment, and in their approach to handling livestock.

Alpine Meadow

High up on a summer range, a cowboy checks the conditions and may pack in salt or mineral blocks to supplement the cattle's steady diet of grass. It is quiet up there, so far away from the end of a dusty dirt road.

The Sea of Grass. This region is the Great Plains, the old buffalo range—a land of which one pioneer said, "You can look farther and see less than at any other place in the world." The plains bump up against the eastern slope of the great Rocky Mountain barrier. Across the mountains, scrub country and deserts are scattered from the Mexican border all the way up into eastern Oregon...and then down the coastal ranges that slope toward the Pacific Ocean.

The heart of the West, the stage upon which the most dramatic episodes of the historical pageant were played out, is the prairie environment of the Great Plains—first, the land of the buffalo; then cow country...a grassy domain for horseback hunters and herdsmen. A government analysis delineated the area as "...728 million acres, nearly 40 percent of the total land area of the continental United States...more than 99 percent is available for livestock grazing."

The area has three basic features. It is, for the most part, relatively flat. There is an absence of trees. Rainfall is not generally sufficient for successful farming. An additional feature associated with the plains is the wind. Except for the seashores, the wind blows more constantly on the plains than any other place in America. Men who ventured here would have had to be tough and resourceful. Nature could be a merciless landlord on the Western frontier.

The American experience, from colonial days up until the mid-nineteenth century, was confined in large measure to the land that lay east of the Mississippi River. Ample rainfall and abundant forests shaped the pattern of frontier life in that region. From Plymouth Rock and Jamestown, all the way to the Mississippi, pio-

On the Way to Carefree

All across the West are remote, primitive places that are just as they have always been, somehow uninviting and yet beautiful.

On the Mogollon Rim

This northern Arizona rim is in a natural cow country. Over the edge, the land falls off to scrub brush and rocky hills and then on to the sprawling desert below and beyond.

neers built log cabins and carved out small farms in the wilderness.

Beyond the big river was a different world. Forests existed in isolated islands, few and far between, except in close proximity to the far-away Rockies. Rainfall was scarce too. The first significant thrust of Americans into the West would leapfrog across the interior plains to the Pacific Northwest, where the familiar components of wood and water where available, or to California, where the lust for gold overrode all other considerations.

Elephant Head (overleaf)

Natural formations such as this one, south of Tucson in the foothills of the Santa Ritas, were landmarks for early travelers on their passage west.

{49}

High Lonesome

A cowboy learns about being alone. It is as much a part of the life today as it was in the old rawhide times. Between the spring and fall roundups, solitary riders roam at an easy pace as they monitor the cattle, check the conditions of essential concerns such as fences and water sources, and scout for better grazing areas or the presence of predators.

Some cowboys relish those times when they are off by themselves. Being outdoors in the West, back away from the roads and clamor of civilization, idle conversation pales in comparison to the early morning birdsong or the nighttime cries of coyotes.

There are those who are marked by the experience of being alone too long. They become uncomfortable in the company of others and are especially ill at ease in town, away from their horses and open skies. People who don't appreciate the solitude of their profession will never understand cowboys.

Arizona Moonlight

There is an amazing quality to moonlight in the Arizona desert. As shapes and shadows shift in the night, old tales of Apache marauders come to mind.

String Lake Outlet, Jackson

*Wyoming wilderness…cool, clear water and shady silence…
secret, peaceful places…untracked and timeless.*

For generations, the vast interior was indicated on maps as the Great American Desert…a mysterious and forbidding place like uncharted corners of faraway seas. The land would determine how men would live out on the plains. The native Americans believed that the land belonged to God, and that its bounty was a blessing. The concept of private ownership of land was unknown to Western Indians. How could you own what was God's? The tribes that followed the buffalo herds were tenants on the land, nature's nomads moving in harmony to the natural rhythm of the seasons. They left few signs of their passage…a scattering of stones at secret, sacred spots, and the crumbling dwellings of the ancient Anasazi.

Then came the cattlemen...a bovine exodus climbing a ladder of rivers north from Texas and spreading out across a vast kingdom of grass. Each river has its own chapter in the cowboy's story, too often told in tragic tones—of death in the dark swirling depths of flood-swollen currents, or mired in the quicksand of boggy banks. Herds were thrown together as far south as the Rio Grande, then driven northward on the dusty trail, crossing rivers whose names evoke emotions like the verses of a Homeric epic: Pecos, Brazos,

Defiance

These were Geronimo's men, as tough and deadly as the land they defended against all who dared to venture there.

Red, Cimarron, Platte, Powder, Belle Fourche, Yellowstone, Tongue, Musselshell and Missouri.

Place names and two-fisted cow towns would forever conjure up

{55}

images of the frontier heritage: Black Hills and Badlands, Llano Estacado, Judith Basin, Big Hole... and Deadwood, Cheyenne, Durango, Adobe Wells, Tascosa and still a hundred more... words on a modern map that resonate with the distant echoes of the warrior's cry and a nightherder's lullaby, each place yet alive side by side with its history... the low hills of Little Bighorn, the narrow dirt streets of Tombstone, Boot Hill in Dodge City's shadow... so many places where men died hard and their spirits do not rest easy.

When the cattlemen came, they learned what the Indian had always understood: that you must adapt to the land, rather than try to change it to suit your own purpose. During the era of the open range, cattle roamed free where the old buffalo trails ran. Nature was quick to assert its sovereignty. Old-time cowmen came to know, the hard way, that it was not all tall grass and pretty sunsets. During the hard winter of 1886–87, the big ranches on the high plains lost up to eighty-five percent of their herds.

Unlike such industries as logging and mining, those involved in cattle-raising did, and still do, take their stewardship of the land as an inviolate trust. Except for fencing, windmills and hay meadows, ranch country looks much as it did a century ago. The character of the range has not been altered in any elemental way, nor will it probably ever be.

Not all those who came west were willing to take the country as they found it, to be grateful in the good years of mild winters and enough rainfall, and to hump up and take it when drought was upon the land or the cold weather hung on too long. The cattleman dreamed big and was willing to play the hand nature dealt him. Many who followed him out onto the plains tried to change the game.

In 1862, President Lincoln signed the Homestead Act, which gave adult citizens the right to claim 160 acres of the public domain. Most of the available land was out West. The people came, on foot or horseback and in long lines of wagons... refugees from crowded cities back East, or worn-out farm country. Their eyes shone with their dreams, but they were unprepared for the peril of an imagined "promised land" where there was very little of milk or honey.

Red Rock Cowboys

One of the most spectacular parts of the Western range country is the area around Sedona in north central Arizona. Tourists awestruck by the scenery may just get a glimpse of cowboys at work.

{57}

Feathers and Spurs

Horses were the common denominator in the cultures of both Indians and cowboys. Warriors and tophands alike were respected for their skills as horsemen. Their tales are told to the tempo of hoofbeats and in the hues of sunlight on horsehide.

The world looks different from the back of a horse. The horseman is superior in a wild environment to those who go about on foot. Good horses were a source of high pride and honor for all those, red and white, whose lives revolved around buffalo and cattle.

Indian horsemen preferred mounts that bore the dramatic patterns and colors of paints, pintos and the Nez Perce pride, the Appaloosa. There was a reverence in the Indian's attitude toward horses. Ceremonial preparations for the hunt, or for war, included painting mystical signs upon favored mounts. Cowboys were more practical in their regard for horses, with a preference for dark solid colors as a general rule. They were as likely to cuss their horses as to praise them.

The Intruders

There were but a few at first... intruders on the buffalo range. The native people watched and wondered as the trickle soon became a torrent.

The homesteaders plowed under native grasses and then watched as the crops they planted withered and the topsoil blew away on the tireless prairie wind. Abandoned homesteads and forsaken dreams littered the land within a single generation. Survival in the West required far-sighted individuals whose vision was bigger than 160 acres.

In 1916, Congress increased homestead allotments to 640 acres. It was still not enough out past the 100th meridian, where rainfall averaged less than twenty inches in a good year. The legacy of dryland farming would play out across the West in the terrible dust-bowl days of the 1930s. A government study prepared in 1936 details the disaster: "Precipitation in the range country averages less than one-third that of the Middle West and East. One to four drought years out of ten characterize practically all of the range area. Most spectacular among the maladjustments of rangeland use has been the attempt to use more than 50 million acres for dry-land farming. About half, ruined for forage production for years to come, has already been abandoned for cultivation."

It was as if nature had decided to punish those who had tried to alter her design. The West is grassland, a place for antelope, coyote and jackrabbits... and a place for cattle and the people who see to their welfare: cow people, attuned by tradition to the natural balance and order of the environment. The land endures. Grass reclaims those spots where audacious men tried in vain to work their will against the unrelent-

Chilson's Place

It is difficult for some people to understand why men would choose to follow the cowboy life in an age of computer technology... and if you ask those who do, they will find it hard to explain. For those who have ventured across this land, it is easier to understand.

ing force of nature. The plowed fields and dwellings of early homesteaders are mostly gone now. But evidence of the indomitable natural process can still be seen. Grass pushes up through the asphalt surrounding deserted service stations and truckstop cafes along empty stretches of Western highways. Weeds flourish in the forlorn shadow of decaying drive-in movie screens at the edge of small Western towns. The prairie wind whistles and moans down the dusty street of a deserted mining town, slowly wiping away the intruders' traces. The land renews itself unto eternity.

The lesson learned by the cattleman is that you must take the land as you find it, synchronize your efforts to seasonal rhythms and responsibly husband the resources of grass and water that nature provides. Then, maybe, if the rains come when you need them and cattle prices hold for awhile longer, it may be possible to

Río Puerco

Up in northern Arizona and across other barren stretches, small rivers and streams such as this meant salvation to thirsty travelers and their livestock. Water in the West is nature's most precious gift.

James Reynolds

nearly break even and stay on the land for another year. It is a tenuous tenancy at best. And if you fight against it, you are bound to lose.

For people not born to it, the West can be an intimidating place. Some are uneasy with the sheer magnitude of open space and the silence that surrounds it all. An early Kansas homesteader eloquently captured the essence of the prairie: "Above their vague and receding horizons forever broods a pathetic solemnity, born of distance, silence, and solitude." An environment that can provoke words such as those is bound to generate an artistic tradition.

Indeed, artists have been there, every step of the way, as America confronted and came to terms with the West. Painters like George Catlin, Karl Bodmer and Alfred Jacob Miller accompanied exploratory expeditions to the West as early as the 1830s, before the white man's mark was upon the land. Frederic Remington and Charles M. Russell captured in their art firsthand impressions of a land in transition, from buffalo range to cow ranch. The list is truly

The Good Life

The irony is clear in this painting's title. Dripping-wet truth dispels the idyllic haze that surrounds our perceptions of cowboys.

a long one of artists who have discovered inspiration in the West.

In the present generation, Western art has most often centered on historical themes, both real and imagined, or representational scenes of contemporary Western life. The art of James Reynolds is an exception. His paintings are highly personal reflections of the influence of the West on his creative sensibilities. He does not paint the oft-told tales of cowboys and Indians. His is a more profound vision: the symbiotic relationship of men, horses, cattle and the land...the harsh and beautiful land.

The figures in a Reynolds painting are not arrogant intruders hell-bent on "winning the West," but solitary riders adrift and unobtru-

{63}

Westward Ho!

What made them leave their world behind and travel to these wild, wasted places? It was in the fabric of who we were, this restlessness to pick up and move on. A symptom of freedom, perhaps: that same kind of impulse that carried colonials out across a broad ocean and then, when securely established in a new land, prompted them to begin the trek ever westward.

Destiny and destination, scrambled together and seasoned with uncertainty and an eternal longing for unknown opportunity and adventure. The wagon wheel is as much a symbol of our heritage as the Liberty Bell or Old Ironsides. Indeed, much of the essential character of America was shaped by the mobility of its people. And there are still those among us for whom moving is the next best thing to being free. Ask a cowboy. He will tell you that the prospect of seeing new country excites him, and it always will, even after he is too old and tired to gather up and go.

Bad News

Overland travel was a hard proposition out beyond the frontier. Disappointment bred disaster when a water source went bad and the next one was a long way down the trail.

A Cold Start

At higher elevations, snow is a possibility during roundups in early spring or in the fall. A ration of grain will fortify the horses for a long, cold day's work. The men will make do with a last cup of hot coffee.

sive in a spaciousness that extends far beyond the margins of the canvas. The paintings are one man's testament of awe and reverence for a place where he belongs.

"I have seen the Arizona desert in the bloom of a wet spring when the colors would rival a tropical rain forest . . . the subtle tones and hues of prairie country beneath an absolutely amazing array of clouds as pure white as the muzzle of a newborn Hereford calf . . . and the wonderful gift of blazing Western sunsets.

"Not long ago, when I was in Wyoming, I had started out before daylight for a meadow outside Jackson Hole. The Tetons were dark shapes against the sky when I first looked. After getting my easel and paint arranged, I glanced up just as the sun hit the high sharp peaks. It was so incredible that I just sat there quietly on the damp ground in sheer awe."

The West is that kind of place, as much today as when man first ventured forth into this big wonderful land that was like no other.

BUFFALO LEGACY: HIDE, HORN AND HOOF

"The sound came first, like rolling thunder. Dust clouds rose high into the sky. . . and then the vanguard of huge, shaggy-headed bulls broke over the crest of a low hill. Behind them came the main herd, strung out for miles and away to the distant horizon. . .pounding hooves, the ebb and flow of synchronized chaos with the power of a thousand tornadoes."

PART III
BUFFALO LEGACY: HIDE, HORN AND HOOF

Yellow Dust

Dust is a constant of cowboy life... blowing dust that will peel off your skin, or dust that just hangs in the air as the herd passes by. Cowboys joke that they can tell what range they are on with their eyes closed, just by the taste of the dust.

The sound came first, like rolling thunder. Dust clouds rose high into the sky. . . and then the vanguard of huge, shaggy-headed bulls broke over the crest of a low hill. Behind them came the main herd, strung out for miles and stretching away to the distant horizon. . . pounding hooves, the ebb and flow of synchronized chaos with the power of a thousand tornadoes. The lion might rule the African veldt, but on the American prairie there was a time when the buffalo truly was the king of beasts.

James Reynolds is intrigued by the buffalo and has observed them from the perspective of an artist, as well as the nostalgic point of view of a romantic.

"There is something fascinating about a buffalo's strange physical shape, particularly when compared to cattle. They seem somehow awkward in their appearance, but not when you see them move. It is very difficult to include them in a composition that is pleasing to my eye. But if you really think about it, the buffalo is probably the most appropriate symbol for the Old West. They represent that time when the Plains Indian was in his full glory. The destruction of the buffalo epitomizes a tragedy that involved so much more than just a problem of wildlife conservation."

It is estimated that sixty million buffalo (American bison) once roamed across North America. Their range extended from the Peace River country in Alberta down into northern Mexico, and from the Continental Divide east into the Virginias. As European settlement moved inland from the south and east, the buffalo withdrew to their natural domain, the Great Plains.

Life for the native Americans of the Plains area was dependent upon the buffalo. Meat, hide, bones, practically every part of the buffalo was utilized by the Plains tribes. The destinies of buffalo and Indian were irrevocably linked. By the 1840s, white men ventured out onto the plains in ever-increasing numbers, and close behind came the railroad. The wholesale slaughter of the great herds began in earnest, and traditional migratory patterns were disrupted forever.

Mare and Colt

Horses are essential to any Western ranching enterprise. They are bred to suit the character of the country and the nature of the work their riders must do. Cowboys will judge an outfit by the quality of its mounts.

{73}

Actin' Up

Good cow horses learn their craft through on-the-job training. Some take to it naturally ...others need the practiced hand of a good rider like this cowboy who has turned his mount away from the herd to refocus the horse's attention.

By midcentury there was a precipitous decline in the number of buffalo, as well as in the quality of life for the native American tribes. The ecological disaster was so extensive that by 1900 perhaps no more than three hundred buffalo still survived in the West, and the proud prairie people were exiled to the squalor of reservations.

But the rain still replenished the plains, and the grass renewed itself each spring. Cowboys and range cattle moved in to occupy the emptiness left by Indians and buffalo.

Cattle, and horses too, were first brought to the New World by Spanish explorers and colonizers. Livestock was off-loaded in the West Indies as early as the 1490s, and on the Mexican mainland in the 1520s. As if in accord with the Old Testament edict, the cattle and horses were fruitful and did multiply. Ranching spread from coastal regions to the interior central highlands, and then northward to the frontier regions of California and Texas.

The seed stock of horses for the Plains Indian came from those

Good Grass

The same prairie grass that sustained the buffalo made the West a suitable country for cattle. Good grass and little rain are the real foundations for beef production.

animals that were lost or stolen or strayed from early Spanish expeditions of discovery, such as the one Coronado led into the American

Against the Sky

Prairie people are intrigued by the mountains that shimmer like beacons on the far horizon. Mystery swirls upon the steep slopes like the clouds that obscure the jagged peaks. Their names conjure up grand images…Bighorn, Beartooth, Bitterroot, Sierra Madre and Sangre de Cristo…labels left by lost wanderers in the wilderness. And legends, too, of desperation and death at terrible places like Donner Pass.

In the mountains, the West clings most tenaciously to its primal character. Time will heal the superficial scars left by hardrock mining and ski resorts, and time to a mountain is a matter of small consequence. There were people aplenty to claim the prairie places, but few men to match the mountains.

Montana de Oro

A mountain is turned gold by the desert sunlight. Natural splendor abounds across the West and is most dramatic in the quiet, lonely places where man has still not left his mark on the land.

{76}

Mystic of the Plains

Mysticism was a major aspect of Plains Indian culture. A warrior sought the blessings of "good medicine" through traditional ceremonial ritual as he prepared for the hunt or for war.

Southwest in 1540. The acquisition of the horse was of tremendous significance to Plains Indian cultures. Horseback hunters and warriors proved to be a formidable barrier to white settlement of the West. Spanish cattle were of little interest to the Indian as long as the buffalo still thrived.

Two separate and distinct livestock-based cultures developed from Spanish origins in California and Texas. Both began with colonization and missionary efforts as early as the 1730s in Texas and 1769 in California. Cattle-raising was a primary focus of the Spanish colonial enterprise in both these regions, as well as to a lesser extent in Florida, New Mexico and Arizona.

The California livestock industry developed and flourished in the isolation imposed by the mountains to the east and an ocean on the west.

Red Rock Country (overleaf)

There are still plenty of places out West where a pickup truck cannot go, and a cowboy has to rely on the old ways. Life in a line camp is lonely, to be sure, and a man better bring with him whatever he will need until spring.

The old California style of ranching would have minimal impact on the broader context of the Western range cattle industry. The environment was similar in many respects to regions of Spain, allowing Spanish style and traditions to retain a purity not observed in other areas.

It was different in other places on the frontier fringes of the Spanish empire. Texas, Arizona and New Mexico did not present the relatively hospitable and familiar environment that was encountered in California. Rough country and hostile Indians were not conducive to pastoral tranquillity. The Spanish efforts in Arizona and New Mexico were limited in scope, but in Texas there was a full-scale attempt to establish a permanent Spanish presence closely tied to cattle-raising.

Nuevo Santander was established as a colonial province along the lower Rio Grande in the 1740s. Here lies the cradle of the Texas cattle-based culture that would ultimately impact throughout the area of the Great Plains. Cattle numbers increased exponentially along the Rio Grande and northward to the Nueces River, not only in the region of Nuevo Santander, but in associ-

Coolin' Down

A cowboy was once asked what he thought about in a quiet, beautiful place like this . . . "Nothing really; I just took it all in and felt happy to be there." Cowboys are about "feeling," not about "thinking."

James Reynolds

Chuck Wagon Ways

There is general agreement that Charles Goodnight outfitted the first chuck wagon for use on the Goodnight-Loving Trail, which he and his partner, Oliver Loving, blazed in 1866. This traveling commissary was the core around which traildrives and roundups operated in a time when fences were few and the grass was free.

Men who took on the job of cooking for a cow outfit constituted a colorful chapter in the saga of the range. Most often they were older men, perhaps cowboys themselves at an earlier time, but now relegated by age and infirmity to a less noble calling. Their temper and bad disposition are legend, and even the boss of an outfit was hesitant to challenge the cook's presumption of authority.

Beef, beans and biscuits...a culinary challenge of small proportion, but a vocation for a crusty character who was willing to wrangle pots and pans in order to stay close to a world that had given his youth some meaning. And on a prairie morning as the wagon rolls along, his thoughts turn to those times when he too was a wild young rider...and his heart aches.

Changing the Wheel Horse

The chuck wagon was the closest thing there was to a home for cowboys on the long trails north to the shipping points, or during roundup seasons on the big range outfits. And the cook was a king on a traveling throne.

ation too with a string of missions that were established to the north and east.

Unlike the conditions in Spanish California, those in Texas demanded innovations in stock management techniques and the vaquero's equipment. The thick, thorny brush made the cattle more elusive and called for a stripped-down utilitarian approach to handling them. Texas vaqueros were pitifully plain in contrast to their stylish California cousins.

When Anglo-Americans began to move into Texas in the 1820s, they found an abundance of wild cattle and horses, the progeny of Nuevo Santander and the old Spanish missions. Mexican independence in 1821, the Texas revolution in 1836 and the Mexican War of 1845 displaced most of the Hispanic ranchers in southern Texas. But traditional methods of stock-raising and the vaquero style were adopted intact by the Anglo-Texans.

During the American Civil War, most Texas cowboys and ranchers went to war. The cattle were left to fend for themselves and they thrived, unbranded and wild. At the same time, the small domesticated herds of Northern and Eastern farmers had been slaughtered to feed the Union army. A demand existed at one end of the country, and an abundant supply at the other end. Horseback visionaries conceived a good enterprise whereby Texas beef would grace the dinner tables of hungry Yankees. If it worked, Texas would escape the economic devastation that characterized the postwar South.

Beginning in 1866, longhorn cattle and Texas cowboys moved out upon the Great Plains. First, to the wild and woolly cow towns of Sedalia, Baxter Springs, Abilene, Ellsworth and Dodge City. And then beyond, to stock the old buffalo range, all the way to the Rockies and northward to, and across, the Canadian line.

Ike Pryor, Texas cowman and traildriver, estimated

Lookin' for Mama

The roundup has gone by, leaving a new calf behind.
The cowboy looks off toward the herd and wonders if the
straggler will go along on his own accord or will
have to be roped and led back to his mother.

{87}

Prelude to Sorrow

*T*he buffalo are almost all gone now. Their bones litter the land, and children cry from hunger in the lodges. There are strangers abroad on the old hunting grounds. They come from the direction where the sun rises, and their passage is marked with scars upon the earth.

Countless generations of native Americans had lived in the western region of America known as the Great Plains. The coming of white men and their responsibility for the decimation of the buffalo herds doomed traditional ways of life for the tribes. The plains would be carved up into farms and ranches, and towns would spring up where tepees had once stood.

Defiance seemed only to harden the resolve of the intruder. After a short span of years, what were not "the old ways" lived only in the memory of a bitter, broken people.

Unwelcomed Tracks

Plains warriors have found the tracks of a white man's wagon. Shall the intruders be allowed to pass, or will their bones be left to bleach under the hot prairie sun?

Winter Calves

Calves born too early are in genuine peril until spring comes. Cowboys are charged with the job of moving them along to a place where there is some shelter from the wind and grass for the hungry mamas.

that, from 1866 to 1895, ten million head of cattle went up the trail: four thousand separate herds averaging 2,500 head each. Pryor said an average of twelve men accompanied each herd and each man had six horses; that twelve to fourteen miles were covered in a typi-

cal day, and that a normal drive of 1,200 to 1,500 miles took three months at a cost of about sixty cents per head. Cattle that were generally worthless in Texas brought twenty to fifty dollars at the Kansas stock pens.

The entire drama of the traildriving era lasted only about twenty-five years. Once Midwestern and Eastern farmers had replenished their herds, the market for Texas beef began to decline. But cowmen had seen the plains; they knew it was nature's most perfect cow range, and the boom shifted to the establishment of ranching. Vast areas of free land and grass lured Eastern and European speculators to enter the open-range cattle business. It seemed so deceptively simple: buy some cattle on credit, or line up investors; then just turn the cattle loose on the public domain, let them multiply, gather the increase and watch the money roll in.

Where there had once been buffalo, now cattle grazed upon a thousand hills and across the broad prairie expanse. By the 1880s, every corner of the plains was crowded with cattle. Overstocking began to impact on the availability of grass and water resources, and prices began to decline as more and more cattle were shipped to market. Frenzied speculation and overcrowding on the range set up the whole of the industry for disaster. The bubble finally burst in the wake of the terrible winter of 1886–87.

It had been dry all summer and into the fall of 1886. November brought fierce storms and blizzards, one after another, as hunger-weakened cattle perished in the deep snow. In February of the new year, temperatures on the northern plains averaged from thirty to forty degrees below zero for a two-week period.

The warm chinook winds finally came in March. When the roundup wagons rolled out that spring, grim-faced cowmen, from the Texas Panhandle to Montana, encountered disaster of an unimaginable scope. Thousands upon thousands of rotting carcasses choked every draw and arroyo. Buzzards swarmed in the skies and swooped down to feast on the remnants of the cowmen's dreams. Many plains outfits lost seventy-five to eighty percent of their herds.

North of Jackson

Old-time trailriders were impressed by the grandeur of great mountains, but they were men more suited to their natural element of open prairies.

Stalking

Death lurked in the shadowy landscape all along the Western trail. Like their brother the wolf, Plains warriors moved fast and silently through the semi-obscured terrain, and tragedy marked the wake of their passing.

The era of the open range had come to an end. Outside investors and speculators were wiped out and bogged in bankruptcy. Nature had once again asserted her dominion over the West. This was the dawn of a new day for cattle-raising on the Great Plains. Henceforth, ranching would be engaged in by families who lived on the land and invested their resources and personal labor in partnership with nature and their creditors.

The new-era cowman would, by deed and lease, restrict his operation to a proscribed piece of the range country. He would learn new methods to conserve and enhance his grass and water supplies, and improve his cattle by breeding up from the rangy old-style Texas stock. Quality rather than quantity would be the new rule on the range.

A hundred years have passed since the rawhide times of traildrives and open ranges, and yet cattle-raising in the West retains much of its original character. Men on horse-back still are the primary care-providers for cattle, and nature's bounty of grass is the sustenance of hope for those who embrace the traditions of the ranching heritage. Today, as always, ranching is a poor living but a rich life. Year-end reports in December 1995 indicated that cattle prices were at a five-year low and were expected to drop even lower in 1996. You have to look at other than economic considerations to find an explanation for the dogged determination on cattle. The "why" of it all is what attracts and holds the interest of an artist like James Reynolds. He touches on the mystery in speaking about that part of the West to which he has become so strongly attached.

"Arizona has always been cow country, and Coconino County is right in the heart of it. Several generations of good cowboys have ridden over this ground. It won't change much for a long time to come. A painting of mine that contains good cattle, good horses and good cowboys brings a smile to the face of anyone who has spent much time on a ranch. There are days when a cowboy wouldn't trade places with any man on earth. The work is hard, the hours are long and the pay is short. But there is a special kind of feeling that comes with being outside and doing a job on horseback. A cowboy couldn't explain it to you very well, but once you have had the experience, you will never forget it."

COWBOYS: THE LAST SAGEBRUSH CAVALIERS

"Most people will go through life without ever having seen a real cowboy. Yet, as with some exotic endangered creature, they have heard rumors of his existence and are intrigued by the stories. Folks who live close to cow country are pleased to report: The cowboy is alive and well. You just can't see him from the Interstate."

PART IV
COWBOYS: THE LAST SAGEBRUSH CAVALIERS

Arizona Cowboys

*Men and horses...eternal symbols of Western tradition, proud stewards
of a living heritage, tied forever to livestock and land, at ease under
open skies and away from the ordinary world.*

The story is told of a titled British gentleman who traveled to a remote Wyoming ranch back in the 1880s when foreign investors were scrambling for a share of the Western beef bonanza. The nobleman was looking for his younger brother, who, due to the strictures of primogeniture, had left England to seek his fortune in the American West. He had secured a job as ranch manager out in the Powder River country.

After a long dusty trip up from Casper, the gentleman arrived in his hired buggy at ranch headquarters. He stopped by the corrals where a lone cowboy was repairing a gate. "I say, my good man, might your master be about?" he inquired. The cowboy's eyes narrowed, and his jaw clinched tight as he turned to face the visitor and replied, "I reckon the boss is up to the big house, but as for 'my master,' I ain't yet met that son-of-a-bitch!"

Therein lies something of the pure and genuine essence of the cowboy. Tough, self-reliant, fiercely independent, prideful . . . all of those tags fit him, and plenty more, too. And it is as true today as it was a century ago. Barbed wire and shorthorn cattle may have changed the *business* of ranching, but the cowboy remains as he has always been, somehow separate and apart from the mainstream.

James Reynolds has been watching cowboys closely for a long time, has ridden with them and devoted a career to portraying them faithfully in their natural element.

"Years ago, when I was still working in Los Angeles, I was driving in the Sierra foothills and stopped at a little country store to get a cold drink. While I was in the store, an old, beat-up, dirty pickup pulled up out in front. Two young cowboys came in laughing and slapping dust off their clothes. Their pantlegs were tucked into their

boot-tops, and they wore spurs that jingled when they walked. They wore brightly colored bandanna wild rags around their necks, and their wide-brimmed hats were sweat-stained dark around the crowns.

"They each bought a beer and then went on out back to bathe in a big metal tub that was fed by a natural hot spring. After about half an hour, they came back in with their hair plastered down, still laughing and talking about horses and women. They bought some hard candy and a couple more beers, and then walked out with their spurs ringing

Almost Home

Cowboys don't have much use for clocks. They arise before dawn and work until the work is done.

on the wooden porch. The old pickup stirred up dust as they pulled back out onto the highway, heading back to the ranch for another thirty days before their next bath and beer break. I felt somehow that

I had just seen something very rare and wonderful."

In the years since, Reynolds has had other opportunities to observe the cowboy in uncontrived surroundings. In 1971, he saddled up and rode along with the IX Roundup in the hills to the east of Big Sandy, Montana. It was an experience that remains vivid for him: long cold days on horseback, listening to the eerie sound of ice popping in the cloven hooves of the cattle, and cold quiet nights huddled in a canvas bed tarp. The feeling was one of being transported to some strange, distant world...a place where you learned things about yourself that you had not known.

Most people will go through life without ever having seen a real cowboy. Yet, as with some exotic endangered creature, they have heard rumors of his existence and are intrigued by the stories. Folks who live close to cow country are please to report: The cowboy is alive and well. You just can't see him from the Interstate.

Those who know about such things will all agree that there is more to the story than the wearing of big

Just in Time

Ranchers try to time their breeding season so that new calves will arrive with springtime. But nature is a capricious mistress, and a late snow can prove deadly for early arrivals. Survival depends on the cowboy.

Hog Heaven

Rain is a blessing in desert country. The thorny plants bloom overnight, and cattle feed on the new grass and become full and content like hogs in a pen.

hats and boots. Teddy Blue Abbott, a Montana cowboy of the open-range era, said, "I believe I would know an old cowboy in hell with his hide burnt off. It's the way they stand and walk and talk." A survey of the autobiographical writings of cowboys tells us about what they did, but little of who they were or why they chose a cowboy's life.

On the other hand, books written about cowboys (rather than *by*

them) present a variety of interpretations and hypotheses, many as arcane as theories relating to the origins of black holes in space. One Eastern writer interviewed an old cowboy a few years ago. The old man was in his eighties and had lived by himself for years in a remote cow camp in the Palo Duro Canyon of North Texas. He told the writer that once a month he rode one of his string of horses thirty miles to visit his wife in town.

The writer was amazed and asked, what did the old man think about during those long rides? The cowboy seemed puzzled at the question and was quiet for awhile. Finally he said, "Well, I don't believe that I think about anything. I just enjoy seeing the country and riding a good horse." That response lies close to the heart of what is the cowboy: a primal need to see the country and ride a good horse.

From a historical perspective, the original cowboy was the vaquero, a product of technique and style transplanted from the Iberian Peninsula and modified according to conditions encountered in the New World. Very few individuals of pure Spanish blood became vaqueros. It was a menial calling, a vocation for Indians and mixed-blood mestizos.

The evolutionary process continued in Texas as settlers from the southern United States moved into the area, beginning in the 1820s. The new Texans brought with them an intact system of livestock husbandry that had been developed with domesticated cattle in wooded regions. This was not an entirely practical approach to stock handling in Texas, where trees were scarce and the cattle were wild.

The Texas cowboy is a fusion of the Anglo-Southern style and the Hispanic vaquero tradition. As cowboys moved out with their herds into the region of the Great Plains, the influence of the vaquero ways was diluted due to the generally open character of the country, as contrasted to the thick brush of southern Texas.

During the century or so since the end of the open range, cowboys have argued endlessly about whether their kind is born or made. In actuality, both positions are correct. There are plenty of cases where

Sage Country

Cowboy conversation tends toward subjects like horses, weather and the latest foolish notion advanced by the owner of the ranch.

James Reynolds
1973 ©

On the Town

Cowboys never got to town very often. But when they did, things were apt to get lively. Young men, daring and virile, craved diversion from the routine of life at the wagon and the company of cows. In the wild old days of wide-open cow towns like Dodge City and Abilene, there was ample opportunity "to see the elephant," as cowboys referred to their sprees.

The first stop in town was usually a barbershop for a haircut, shave and a bath in a back-room tub. Then, with a clean shirt and hair slicked down, they strode out with spurs a-jingling on board sidewalks in search of whiskey, cards and, perhaps, the trail town's version of female companionship.

Brief, reckless interludes…then back to camp or the trail, and the dim, hazy recollections that would become part of the cowboy legend.

The Supply Wagon

These men are headed for town and a break in the routine of ranch life. Their pace coming back will be a slow walk as they relive a full night's adventure.

Spring Showers (overleaf)

Rainfall is a precious commodity in cow country. Without it, the grass will wither and die, and the cattle will go hungry. Spring showers can bring a smile to the face of the most hardened cowman.

{105}

the sons and grandsons of cowboys have clung to their horseback heritage. But it cannot be anything connected to the promise of wealth that makes boys take up their fathers' saddles. Cowboy wages have never amounted to much, and they still don't: about $500 per month in the present day. A lot of good hands have moved to town, especially the married ones, and sought other work because of financial considerations. Age takes a toll, too . . . bad horses and rough living can make a man old beyond his years. But it is a heritage hard to ignore. Those born to it will forever find it hard to walk away.

But some do, and for every cowboy who hangs up his spurs, someone else will show up at roundup time looking for a riding job. It might be a long-haired kid from town looking for an acceptance he never found at home, a whiskey-soaked derelict in search of sanctuary or a bright-eyed refugee from back East who bought into the myth of Saturday matinees and John Wayne. The motives are as many and as varied as the boys and men themselves. A precious few will fit the life and go on to replenish the ranks of riders who know that their welfare is less important than that of the cattle they tend.

The whole thing about cowboys is not nearly so complicated as the romantics and

The Henry

The first of the Winchester repeating rifles was the Henry. This one, held aloft in defiance or as an entreaty to the spirits, was obtained at the cost of its original owner's life and will now be used against others of his kind.

{108}

Duane

Cowboys, like the horses they ride, come in all shapes and sizes and colors. Their commonality has to do with the work and the pride they share, and the heartfelt conviction that they are a part of something that will never be ordinary.

Monsoon

Old-timers call the seasonal spring and fall rains "monsoons" down in the desert portions of southern Arizona. The land blooms overnight into a lush and colorful panorama and is a delight to see for ranchers who have grown weary of dry weather and hungry stock.

Arizona

The natural wonders of the West rival those to be found anywhere on earth. Arizona alone embraces an amazing variety of scenic splendor, from its southern desert desolation to the soaring mountains and coniferous forests in the north. Then too, there are the canyons that trace the meandering tracks of ancient waterways...steep shadowy gorges through which the ghosts of Apache marauders seem still to pass in silent single file.

Crown jewel among all of Arizona's environmental wonders is the Grand Canyon, which stretches spectacularly over two hundred miles along the course of the wild Colorado. No one who has stood at the rim and looked out across the abyss is likely to forget the drama of that moment. All who have come here have shared the common experience of being in awe at the majesty of such a sight.

Canyon Rim

It is still possible, out West, to stand in spendid isolation surrounded by silence and to behold nature's wonders...vistas of sky and space beyond imagining.

Alex Grant Swaney

A friend of the artist, of whom he writes…
"Cavalry soldier, cowboy and poet…a gentle man with
a passion for the West and the people who met its
challenge. Truly, the last of a breed."

historians have made it out to be. To be a cowboy involves not much more than a reasonable level of competence in doing a job of work involving horses and cattle. It is about what you can do, rather than how you feel about it or how it appears to others. For cowboys, what you do is who you are. A cowboy may have the

Steppin' Out

After a long trot from camp, the cowboys pause
to tighten saddle cinches in preparation for another
long day during roundup.

Winter Moonlight

The cold seeps clear down into a man's bones on a moonlit winter night, and his horses can feel it too. Cowboy thoughts turn to summertime memories and the smell of coffee boiling on an open fire.

soul of a poet or be a complete dullard, but it is his skill at the work that validates his credentials as a cowboy.

If our ideas about the cowboy somehow miss the mark, it is because we have known him only from afar and through the eyes of others...and not in the actuality of his natural element, at work, doing those very things that define him.

"Four o'clock in the morning, dark, and a cold wind blowing as the cook rattles his pans and gets the fire going. Men pulling on their boots and listening for the sound of the horses coming in...a cup of hot coffee, but no greasy breakfast for that one boy who is worried about staying on the horse that is up in his string today.

"Sun moving higher now, and cattle spilling off the hills down unto the flat...dust rising, and the constant bellow and bleat of cows and calves searching frantically for each other in the crowded confusion. Quick, sure loops on calf hocks, dallies around the saddlehorn and a fast trip to the branding fire, where the smell of blood and burning hair drifts off on the midmorning breeze.

"Coffee again and a cold bite of something plain, then saddle cinches tugged tight on a fresh horse and work enough to last past dark.

"Half a day of spring roundup, two days down and at least two more still to go before the wagon moves on to another camp...the cook needs a drink bad and is getting mean; one man hauled to town with a broken leg after his horse spooked and fell with him crossing a rocky stretch. The evening camp is mostly quiet now, everyone tired and nursing assorted aches and pains from wrestling healthy calves at the fire...high overhead in the clear night sky, the faint sound and blinking lights of a jet...no one wonders where it is going; it has nothing at all to do with them. Hell, anyone can ride on an airplane."

ROUNDUP: TRAIL DUST AND PROUD MEMORIES

"There is a shared bond between those who wore feathers and those who wore spurs . . . lives forever linked to the land and the memory of great grazing herds. Cowboys are the heirs to the wild places, not unfeeling interlopers but simply another generation of stewards for the prairie grasslands."

PART V

ROUNDUP: TRAILDUST AND PROUD MEMORIES

Cold Country, Hot Coffee

Life in a roundup camp is hard, without doubt. But there have always been men who were made for it. Cold mornings can test a cowboy's resolve and cause him to linger a bit longer for one more shot of coffee before he rides away.

s the millennium approaches, cowboys cling to traditions, adrift and apart in a world marked by change. Their life is still defined by their work, and the nature of that work is essentially as it has always been…the horseback husbandry of beef cattle. James Reynolds can testify to the constancy of Western ways: "To hear someone casually remark that the West is dead is not an uncommon occurrence these days. Many people have the impression that the horse-and-cowboy style of ranching has disappeared in the face of modern technology. I have to challenge that. There have been changes in the past hundred years, but when it gets right down to the job of managing the welfare of cattle in big country, there is only one sure way to do it. And that is with a good cow horse and a good cowboy sitting on top of him. It is a tried and true partnership, and eloquent proof that the West survives."

Indians, horses and buffalo…cowboys, horses and cattle: nature's choice of tenants for the wonderful country that is the West. There is a shared bond between those who wore feathers and those who wore spurs…lives forever linked to the land and the memory of great grazing herds. Cowboys are the heirs to the wild places, not unfeeling interlopers but simply another generation of stewards for the prairie grasslands.

Two time-worn axioms of the range country encompass the primary aspects of cowboy philosophy. The first is: *A man afoot is no man at all*. For it is the horse that elevates the cowboy, literally and figuratively, and sets him apart from those who go about on foot.

Dignity attaches to the man on horseback, and the implied mobility afforded by horses has meant freedom to the restless, wandering spirits of generations of cowboys.

The second tenet of cowboy philosophy is: *The horseman always rides beside an open grave*. This is the acknowledgment that danger and death are twin shadows loose in the land of the horseman. Cowboy life can exact a hard toll from those who choose it. But

Summer Shadows

Summer work for cowboys means moving the cattle, in search of ungrazed areas of new grass.

choose it they do, with an appreciation for the raw-edged intensity that underlies it all. In a letter to a friend, one old crippled-up cow-

One Man's Family

A dog is good company for a lone cowboy here in search of stray cattle that were missed in the roundup.

puncher wrote: "I wish I had have never saw a cow ranch. Probably I would not have had to have been cut on and suffered so much. Too many bad horses has been the cause of most of my troubles. While I'd rather be on a cow ranch and work for just wages, be well, have good health, than anything you could name. When you grow up to anything 'tis hard to quit and have to try something else...."

There is a tempo and temperament that goes with a life lived around cow camps and on ranches. It is keyed to the seasonal rhythms of the work. Just as ducks are drawn southward at the approach of winter, cowboys have an instinctual need to be there and mounted up when the roundup wagon rolls out for branding in the spring or shipping in the fall.

Away from their own kind, in town and among strangers, cowboys are ill at ease and awkward. Boot heels and bowed legs rob a cowboy on foot of the natural grace that marks him when he is in the

saddle. Idle talk does not come easy either. There is not much to talk about with people who are not attuned to the cycles of weather and grass and cattle. "There's too damn much talk in town" is a common complaint of men who have learned to listen in remote places where noise is unnatural.

Cowboy pride is easily mistaken for arrogance by those who are strangers to a life where men cultivate a stoical disregard for emotional and physical discomfort. Town folks are likely to take offense at the cowboy's austere indifference. Back home, while visiting old friends and family, a seasoned cowboy is likely to excuse himself

A Strange Sign

The war lance and a white man's hat tell the tragic tale. An intruder's bones will bleach beneath the prairie sun.

from the clatter of suppertime and wander outside to sit alone on the porch and watch the sky. And when in town he may end up in a dark barroom drinking alone.

Cowboy life somehow renders a man incapable of ordinary social discourse outside his own circle. Saddest of all is the circumstance of

Mountain Moods

*O*ld tales are told in the shadow of Western mountains. Legends of lost treasure guarded by the vengeful spirits of haughty conquistadors and bloodthirsty bandits. And the stories of secret, sacred places where the ancient ones lived in dwellings carved into cliffsides. There is mystery in the mountains, high up where the eagles nest and lightning flashes within the dark mass of distant thunderheads.

We are drawn to and, at the same time, intimidated by mountains. They distort our sense of scale and resist our feeble attempts at intrusion. To the pioneer overland travelers, the mountains were an unforgiving barrier: great rocky obstacles upon whose barren slopes dreams were dashed and despair marked the trail.

Snake River, Jackson

Cowboys wonder how anyone who has seen sights such as this could ever be content to live in a city. They crave the wild places of mountains and sky and the lonesome sound of a coyote's call.

a cowboy incapacitated by injury or age, cut loose from the only kind of life he has ever known and exiled to town for endless bleak days and nights in a spare room in the home of a reluctant relative. Desolate and despairing, he sifts through old horseback memories as his pride seeps away a bit at a time. He is left with little else but those memories and the absolute conviction of having been a part of something that gave his life meaning... something now lost to him.

The story is told of a hardscrabble cowman, a bachelor, old and infirm, living out his last days in the bedroom of a ranch house that has been his home for half a century. A preacher from town, a persistent proselytizer, visits the old man with promises of salvation and choirs of angels singing at the gates of heaven. The old man sends him away and asks a cowboy to gather a bunch of cattle and hold them in the corrals located close to the house. It is done as he asked, and the cowboy returns to the dying man's bedside. The noise of bawling cattle can be heard loud and clear through the open bedroom window. The cowboy asks, what is he to do with the cattle? The old man says, "Hold 'em awhile. I want to go out with that sound in my ears. Who that has heard a bull beller down a canyon would want to listen to the singing of a bunch of pasty-faced angels?"

A stereotypical character in the novels and films that presume to portray cowboys is the querulous old camp cook. This characterization reflects a range-country reality, although the novelist or screenwriter may not have understood its origins. The job of cook often fell to an older man who had previously earned a rider's wages but was no longer able to do a job on horseback. Unwilling to turn his back on a life that has forsaken him, he grasps at the single opportunity that will allow him to remain

Swing Shift

Sundown, the herd close by shifting and settling after a long day on the trail. A lone cowboy sits on a fresh young colt, alert to the movement of the cattle... a couple of hours on night guard, then the refuge of camp and a chance to bed down beneath a broad canopy of stars.

close to the only world he knows. The popular rendition presents him as a comic figure: cranky, ill-tempered and the butt of cowboy jokes. In truth, he is a tragic figure, relegated to a menial job involving pots and pans amidst other men who use rope and spurs. He was once one of them, proud and sure . . . and now each morning as the sun breaks over the horizon, the men ride out and he is left alone and afoot with a dirty apron tied about his waist and a washtub full of greasy cups and plates.

Nostalgia colors the cowboy's world with tints and hues of yesterdays. Old men sit and tell tales of how it once was when they were young and wild. Young men cinch their saddles on broncs and ride out in rough country with ropes tied hard and fast to the horn, all the while lamenting the fact that they were not born a hundred years earlier. It is a life where boys grow up fast, and men turn old too soon. The work and weather wear on a man and toughen him from the outside in.

And in the evenings, like old-time whaling men in a waterfront tavern or Vikings on a forlorn north-country coast, the cowboys gather around the fire, telling tales of men and horses and how it used to be . . . wild rovers all, looking backward through time for meaning and substance in their calling. Stories

Catalina Roundup

These cowboys are working a small bunch in the foothills around Tucson, Arizona. The feeling of a good horse under you on just such a day can mark a man for life and make everything else seem hollow.

about Charlie Siringo, Teddy Blue and Tom Blasingame; of Colonel Goodnight's Palo Duro outfit, Print Olive's hardcase crew up in the sand hills, and the tough Arizona country where cowboys were as wild as the cattle they chased in Bloody Basin. No thought at all for the future beyond tomorrow morning and the horse that is up in your string. And then soon, too soon, the campfire burns down to

Trespassing

Prairie warriors pause at the sight of a distant emigrant camp. The land is theirs, and the tale will tell out the tragedy.

Sierras

The range plays out at the approach to mountains. This is the slope of the Sierras, south of Reno, Nevada.

embers . . . glowing like the memories of the men who had been there before.

How different it is than what Hollywood would have us believe. Silver saddles and six-gun sagas are as alien to cowboy reality as roses and lace. The list of things that really matter to a cowboy is a short one: an outfit to work for that respects tradition . . . good horses to ride and open country to ride them

{133}

The Outfit

A cowboy's possessions are few and generally limited to implements related to his job. Taken together, they are called his "outfit." While it varies from man to man, a typical outfit will include: a saddle and saddle pads or blankets; a couple of ropes, around thirty feet in length for most cowboys, but up to sixty feet for high-desert buckaroos; an assortment of bridles, including a variety of bits and a hackamore to suit the particular differences in the horses in his string; a pair of spurs and a set of hobbles; a canvas tepee and poles along with a bedroll and a small sack of extra clothing, including a brush jacket and a heavy coat; a pair of chaps, a couple pairs of boots and a couple of high-crowned, wide-brimmed hats, one for work and one for town. Most of these items can be rolled up and carried in his bed, or in a catchall called a "war bag."

"Outfit" may be used in a broader sense to designate a ranching operation and all it encompasses, or a roundup crew, along with the remuda of horses and the chuck wagon.

Catch Pens

All creatures, cowboys included, seek the company of their own kind. People who are not familiar with the life cannot understand the quiet pride that exists among men who share the horseman's heritage.

{135}

in . . . and the company of others like himself, men you can depend on in a crunch: men, as they used to say, who would do to ride the river with.

The priorities have not changed all that much through several generations of cowboys, and they are not likely to for as long as people crave beef and grass grows upon the Western lands. And those who have known the life, or even rubbed up against it, are marked forever in some subtle manner that sets them apart from other men. The marks are more prominent on some . . . stooped, graying men with a fire in their eyes that belies age and infirmity. Others carry their hurt in their hearts, grieving quietly for long-ago days, the feel of a good horse between your legs and the eternal attraction of what lies beyond the distant hills.

In 1943, Carl Benedict, who had cowboyed in the Texas Panhandle back in the 1890s, wrote these words

First Lesson

The spring roundup is when the new calves are roped and dragged for branding. Heel loops instead of head loops prevent choking the calves, and a good roper is an asset for any outfit. The title refers to the calf's introduction to the ways of men.

Uneasy Alliance

A cowman runs his ranching operation in partnership with tight-fisted, cold-eyed creditors and a whimsical Mother Nature. The unpredictable combination of weather, animal health, feed costs, consumer demand for beef, market price, availability and cost of credit, and a myriad of other intangible and intractable factors figures into the equation.

Without other sources of income or the discovery of oil on his range, about the best a cowman can hope for is to break even over a long span of years. A cowman was once asked what he would do if he had all the money in the world. He thoughtfully replied, "I guess I'd apply it against my debt as far as it would go." In the modern day, the burden has grown heavier. Cowboys are content to have a riding job, and few aspire to the weighty responsibility that comes with proprietorship.

Orphans

Twin calves are a rare sight. The stress of multiple births and cold weather may have proven too much for the mother cow. The cowboys will each take a calf across the front of their saddles and carry them back to the ranch, where they can be cared for.

Baby Sittin'

Playing nursemaid is not such a bad job if you have a good horse under you and wide-open country.

The Holding Pens

The morning's gather has reached the pens where the new calves will be separated from their mothers and branded. It is a dusty, dirty business.

{141}

An Old Friend

The memory remains vivid: springtime on the trail, lightning flashes on a dark night and the wild rush of cattle in full stampede...and the dreadful sight of a horse and rider going down among the leaders...going down for good.

in his reminiscences: "For a long time I did not see any of the boys that worked up there. Some of them I have never seen again. I have never been back to that country, and do not want to go back, because it would be painful to me to see the open prairies where we used to throw the roundups together, now cut up into farms, and to hear farmers' cowbells jingling in the Pease River breaks where once we chased the big, free steers."

James Reynolds understands and shares the cowboy kind of disaffection for the modern age and what other people call "progress." His home in Sedona once sat alone amidst the sandstone and sage. Today, houses crowd in on all sides, and an outlet mall is just down the road. Reynolds has moved on, south, to a scrub desert rim outside Phoenix. He looks down on the urban sprawl and dirty air and remembers a different Arizona, thirty years ago, and Montana, too, before they became homogenized with fast-food franchises and Wal-Marts.

He remembers the horses...most of all the horses, and the men and the open country. His saddle sits in a shadowy corner of his artist's studio, unridden and dusty now as he toils at his easel, preserving his memories on canvas so that we all might share them.

JAMES REYNOLDS: COWBOY AT HEART

"I believe that my understanding of Western reality has strengthened my art. I was, like most people, drawn to cowboys as a result of the myth. But it is the reality that has sustained and held my interest, and been the inspiration for my art."

PART VI

JAMES REYNOLDS: COWBOY AT HEART

The Freighter

Commerce was a makeshift proposition on the old
Western frontier. Distribution depended on horsepower and
a hardy breed of men who were willing to undergo the
hardship and peril of a wild, lonely land.

James Reynolds takes Western subject matter beyond the traditional limitations of the cowboy-and-Indian genre. His work is distinguished by an honest, uncontrived approach to Western reality, tempered with the soft edges of impressionism. He paints not only what he sees, but also how he feels about what he sees. "I have been asked many times over the years to express my feelings about my work. This has always been difficult for me. I find it much easier to express myself in my painting rather than in words. Some artists expound on the spiritual aspect of their work, their quest for immortality or how they were led by some unseen source of inspiration to produce their ultimate masterpiece. I lay claim to none of this nonsense. I simply want to interpret, in my own way, what I see, in a manner that is both pleasing and harmonious. My reasons for what I do come down to a few basic considerations: my love of nature and of beautiful things, and my training. My only quest is to share those feelings with those who see my work."

It is fortunate for Western culture that James Reynolds chose to devote his career as an artist to Western subject matter. His work is a significant contribution to a rich cultural heritage. Inspiration for the artist abounds all across the West, from the far bank of the Mississippi River to the Pacific shore. There is magnificence in the great mountains, and subtle beauty in the prairies and deserts. And there are the people: native American faces etched with dignity and despair, and the proud progeny of pioneers whose lives were molded by the frontier challenge. James Reynolds was born to it all, a native son of the West. His art is a celebration of his birthright.

Childhood memories are a part of the power that shaped the artist James Reynolds would become. Many of the most vivid recollections

revolve around the small rustic settlement called Washington, California . . . away from the urban sprawl of Los Angeles, inland, up among the foothills of the towering Sierras, in a time of somehow sunnier days before World War II changed California forever.

Reynolds's grandmother operated an old ramshackle hotel that had been built during the gold rush days when dreamers descended like a plague of locusts to pan for riches in the swift currents of the Yuba River. The main road through town, still unpaved in Reynolds's

The Summit

Time falls away in the Western wilderness, and a solitary rider knows the privilege of his calling.

childhood, was the very same track taken by the desperate survivors of the ill-fated Donner Party when they came down out of the mountains after that tragic winter of 1846–47.

Diamond-A Cowboy

*Brands are the heraldry of the range. This cowboy is proud
to ride for the cow outfit that brands the Diamond-A.*

The world was still innocent back in those long summer days of
the 1930s, particularly for a small boy who got away from the city for
sunshine seasons of adventure, roaming in the hills along the river
and exploring the hidden places still haunted by the uneasy spirits of
long-dead gold seekers. And out on the porch of the old hotel in the
evening, the boy listened to the tales told by old men: stories of
golden bonanza, of rough, two-fisted hard cases, and the violence
and bloodshed that went with the life in gold country. After dark, the
boy would lie awake listening to the sound of an old piano in the
downstairs saloon and the dull rumble of old-timers drunk on whiskey and memories.

Sixty years later, those summers still shine for James Reynolds.

He was marked by those days with a lifelong love of the outdoors, an
abiding interest in the drama of Western history and a sensitivity to
the natural beauty of uncrowded Western places. These are facets of
his talent, every bit as important as his command of the brush and
palette. These are things you cannot learn in art school, but which are
essential to the creation of art that achieves a quality beyond technical competence…things of the soul, rather than the hand and the eye.

A single, ordinary incident provided the spark that fired James
Reynolds's interest in and inclination toward fine art. At the age of
thirteen, he was given a calendar by his mother. On that calendar was
the reproduction of a Western painting by Frank Tenney Johnson.
The picture fascinated the boy. It had horses in it and a Western landscape, both of which appealed to him. But he sensed something
more, something a step further from a photographic image…the
"something" that is art. Young Jim Reynolds held on to that calendar
long after the year it recorded had passed. Frank Tenney Johnson and
that calendar were the genesis of Reynolds as an artist.

Frank Tenney Johnson (1874–1939) studied in New York under Robert Henri and William Merritt Chase. He traveled extensively throughout the West and ultimately made his home in California. His style of painting used color to establish mood and was quite different from that of most of his contemporaries, who favored the more literal realism of traditional techniques of illustration. The impact of Johnson's work was a prominent force in the development of James Reynolds's approach to his own painting. His admiration and respect for Johnson are undiminished by the passage of time.

American boys coming out of high school in the 1940s were much more intent on getting into the war than thinking about career paths. For Reynolds, the dream inspired by the Frank Tenney Johnson calendar was packed away along with the childhood memories of the old hotel at Washington. He enlisted in the navy and served in the Pacific theater as a crewman on landing crafts deployed in several invasions. Like a lot of boys, James Reynolds grew up during the war and would reenter civilian life with a seasoned maturity and resoluteness.

On the long voyage home at war's end, young men crowded together aboard ship and passed endless days and weeks of boredom with talk about hopes and dreams for their futures. One of Reynolds's messmates had a small paint set and shared its meager contents with the sailor who still remembered that old calendar picture. Out there somewhere on the broad ocean, homeward bound, James Reynolds experienced epiphany. He knew, with absolute conviction, that he would be an artist.

Back home in California, Reynolds utilized his G.I. benefits and enrolled at the School of Allied Arts in Los Angeles. The school was operated by Stan Parkhouse, who had been a successful New York illustrator in the manner of Howard Pyle, N.C. Wyeth and Harvey Dunn. For four years, Reynolds absorbed all that Parkhouse had to offer on the rich tradition associated with such Eastern art schools as Coopers Union and the New York Art Students League. He could not have known it then but that tradition was dying, and he would be in the last generation to receive an education steeped in the fundamentals. The advent of television was revolutionizing classical advertising art and commercial illustration, and the formlessness of new approaches to fine art seemed to render classical standards of beauty and taste no longer appropriate.

Upon the completion of his formal education with Parkhouse, Reynolds found a job in Southern California's booming aircraft industry, doing production and technical illustration. It was not ful-

Men and Horses

The explanation for our continuing fascination with cowboys is not clearly discernable within a context of reality. James Reynolds has seen that world and knows it to be made up of unremarkable men doing a tough job for meager wages: nothing exceptional at all...except for the presence of horses.

Reynolds has said, "I think it has to do with the image of a man on a horse. There is something appealing and eternal there—an implication of power and nobility. And it has always been so: the masses of people on foot in awe of the few on horseback.

"It is how we perceive cowboys, rather than the cowboys themselves, that is the source of our fascination. They seem wild and free to us, in stark contrast to our own ordinary lives. Men on horses rode through my dreams when I was a child...and they still do today."

filling work. By now he had come to know and appreciate the creative process. He longed to use his talent and abilities to create personal statements in art, rather than schematic renderings of aircraft components. He quit his job and moved up north to a small farm near Porterville. Here he raised rabbits and chickens, gave art lessons, painted what was in his heart, mostly Western scenes... and in the process came close to starving. But talent and purpose are forged in the fires of hardship and struggle.

In 1954, Reynolds returned to Los Angeles and went to work for motion-picture studios, including Fox, MGM, Columbia and Disney. He did set sketches, production illustration, continuity work, titles and anything else they threw at him. His workdays belonged to the studios for more than a dozen years, but on his own time, he painted for himself. The dream persisted...of fine art and the images of men and horses and wide-open spaces.

Reynolds's Western paintings began to sell for modest prices in a few small California galleries. In 1960, he began a long relationship with Bill O'Brien, who operated a gallery in Scottsdale, Arizona. He moved in two worlds: one marked by the demanding frenzy of the movie studios, and the other alone at his own easel, working toward the goal of getting down his personal impressions of the West and creating a niche for himself in the world of fine art.

By 1967, Reynolds was confident enough to flee the morass of Hollywood for the welcome isolation of northern Arizona. He settled on a piece of land outside the small town of Sedona, amidst the spectacular red rock formations that stood out against a blue sky that was dazzling in its clarity. He knew with an absolute certainty that this was where he belonged.

Within a year of coming to Arizona, Reynolds had become a prominent figure in the vanguard of a cultural phenomenon. Contemporary Western art was emerging as the most dynamic segment of the American art scene. What was previously a Southwestern regional genre had, almost overnight, developed an international following. Much of the focus of attention was on the work produced by the two dozen members of a loosely organized group called the Cowboy Artists of America. All four founders of the group lived in Arizona, two of them right in Sedona, where Reynolds was. He accepted membership in 1968 and began to exhibit his paintings at the annual group show at the National Cowboy Hall of Fame in Oklahoma City.

Cowboy Artist, Cowboy Hall of Fame, and the cowboy paintings of James Reynolds...like some fortuitous alignment of stars that promises the grace of good fortune. And so it was. For the next

dozen years, Reynolds competed in the public arena like a bronc rider at the rodeo where the adrenaline flows freely and your reputation is on the line each time the chute gate swings open... Oklahoma City, Phoenix, Dallas, Houston, until the distractions began to interfere with his ability to concentrate on what he believed was most important: the doing of the work, rather than all that had come to surround its presentation and sale.

In 1979, Reynolds hung up his Cowboy Artist's spurs and sought the sanctuary of his studio to refocus and concentrate on his personal artistic priorities, rather than those of others who were caught up in the stampede that Western art had become. But he left the arena as a winner, with a long string of exhibition awards to his credit, and the respect of his peers. Opening night at galleries and museum venues for contemporary Western art had, for a time, come to resemble the trading floor of a commodities exchange. Reynolds was uncomfortable in an environment in which money and hype had

Taos Lady

Little remains for her but the memories etched in her soul like the lines on her face: bright days at the pueblo, tall corn growing, the smell of woodsmoke and the laughter of happy children who were her own.

Neil Kayquoptewa

Proud heir to the traditions and culture of the Hopi people of Third Mesa. A friend to strangers who come with respect and reverence for the old days, including an artist, James Reynolds.

become more important than artistic integrity. He retreated to his studio determined that if he was going to play the Western art game, it would be on his own terms.

For Reynolds, this was a period of reassessment and renewal. He would devote all his energies to painting; everything else would have to take care of itself. Except for a few private commissions, Reynolds would restrict his public exposure to a single, one-man exhibition each year at the same gallery in Scottsdale where Bill O'Brien had given him his first break back in 1960.

For nearly ten years (1979–1988), James Reynolds shunned the spotlight, seeking something more profound and lasting. He calls that which he sought "the step further," something beyond mere competence and the complacency it breeds. Introspection led to a

{153}

Leftovers

Navajo travelers share the remnants of a meal and prepare to move on . . .
leftovers of scant provisions, and the people themselves, leftovers of a time
when all the world seemed their own.

seasoned maturity in Reynolds's painting, as well as his understanding of the creative process. "Art cannot be casual. I have learned the value of discipline and hard work, and that doing it right takes time. I have discarded set patterns and formulas. My approach to painting changes, although I realize the need to be bold, rather than tentative. I have also come to appreciate that there are both technical and emotional considerations in the creation of worthwhile art. The West—its landscapes and characters—will always figure prominently in my work, but I believe aesthetics are more important than historical fidelity or authenticity. The subject matter is secondary to the art: how it is done, rather than what it is about."

James Reynolds is a lot like the cowboys he paints . . . tied hard and fast to the truth and beauty of Western reality, persevering in spite of the misconception of those who regard him from afar . . . content in a calling forever linked to the freedom of horses and open country.

LIST OF PAINTINGS